O9-BTJ-931

Contents

Introduction

As a first-time mom, I found myself swimming in a sea of hormones, sleep deprivation, and questionable Internet advice. Each parenting article was always accompanied by a stock photo of a glowing mother and chipper baby surrounded by endless bowls of fruit and salad in an immaculately clean house. I stared bleary-eyed, with my red-faced baby, at their embodiment of maternal perfection and wondered, "Why don't *we* look like that?"

In spite of my frustration, I decided to rise above it and focus my energy on positive personal growth. Just kidding! I decided to make fun of it to make myself feel better. And it worked! And it turns out it worked for millions of people all over the world: One fateful day, a Facebook thread where frustrated moms were posting idealized photos depicting life with children caught my attention. I started adding sarcastic captions to the photos, someone said, "This should be a blog," and I volunteered. That is how my Tumblr blog, "It's Like They Know Us," was born. Then, overnight, my very public coping mechanism went viral. Over a million people visited in the first month. Soon it was featured on *The Steve Harvey Show, The Huffington Post,* and WNYC's *The Longest Shortest Time.* I was even invited to be a guest on the *Today* show. I got to stay overnight in a hotel by myself and have my hair and makeup done by professionals, and no one threw up on me, or pooped on me, or tried to pull my shirt down in public even once! And now my very public coping mechanism has become a book.

So, come and lose yourself in a white-and-beige utopia where pregnant women always smile, babies always sleep, and toddlers sit perfectly still. Marvel at teenagers who smile adoringly as their parents speak. Extra how-tos and advice columns will help you re-create the same pristine existence in your own home! Congratulations on your purchase of this book and for taking the first steps of your journey on the road to perfection.

Perfecting Pregnancy

Congratulations on your happy news!
Take this time to prepare for your new life
by getting lots of uninterrupted sleep, making your home
baby friendly with all-white furniture, and reading as
much on the Internet as possible. Pregnancy is the first
of *many* opportunities you will have to be absolutely
confident in every decision you make for your child!

Catching a beautiful
sunrise is easy when
you're up every
12 minutes to pee.

"Aw, we are *totally* prepared for this."

"I just peed a little when I laughed!"

"That's okay, I just farted. Let's keep walking."

7

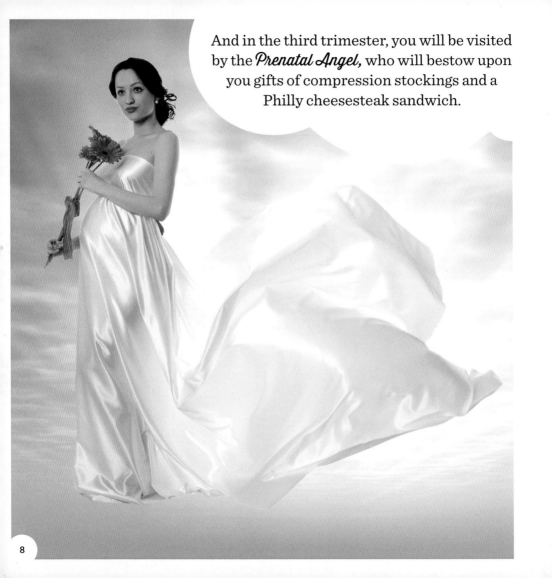

And in the third trimester, you will be visited by the *Prenatal Angel,* who will bestow upon you gifts of compression stockings and a Philly cheesesteak sandwich.

"I always see my regular doctor, and I never feel rushed during appointments. The clipboard lets me know *it's science.*"

At *two months* pregnant, you may decide to wait a bit longer before spreading your happy news. That way those around you can enjoy all of the hormonally induced rage with none of the context!

Known for their nimbleness, agility, and endless lung capacity, many pregnant women find that 90 minutes of regulation soccer is a *great way* to stay fit.

"Thank you for your help putting the crib together. I value your opinion. This is going smoothly."

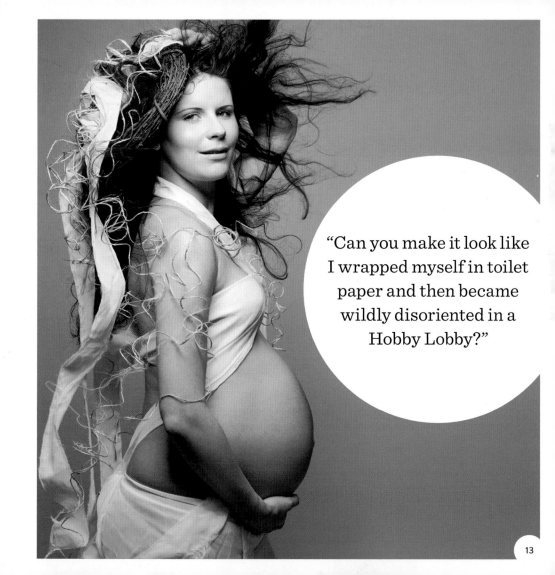

"Can you make it look like I wrapped myself in toilet paper and then became wildly disoriented in a Hobby Lobby?"

The third to fourth month of pregnancy is a *great time* to exhaust friends and family members by obsessing over whether you "actually *look* pregnant" or just "like you got kind of fat."

"Time for
another busy day
at the office!"

15

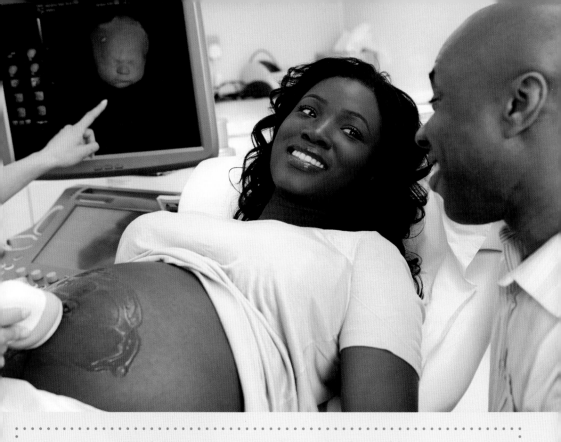

"And there you can see the perfectly visible, unobstructed face. You can tell because it looks exactly like an *adorable little baby face* and not a horrifying 3-D smooshed-pumpkin monster that will haunt your dreams for the next three weeks."

"Oh, absolutely! I *love* that you are doing that right now. I am public property."

Month six is a great time to kick back on some *porous volcanic ocean rock* and chug a nice big bottle of milk in the sun.

"Put on your best crop top, babe.
We're going to CVS to cradle some apples."

Everything about having a baby is going to be clean and quiet and *pretty*.

Month seven is a great time to take advantage of your excellent center of balance and endless energy. Try a new hobby, like *salsa dancing!*

"Nothing to worry about here. Looking it up online *always* puts my mind at ease."

"HAHAHAHA! Of *course* I know what to buy my baby! I am not careening into an overstimulated first-time-parent anxiety spiral in the middle of Babies'R'Us."

"Guess which one of us is peeing a little right now.
That's right—*all of us.*"

Eating Healthily While Pregnant

Use the best ingredients possible when cooking that bun in the oven! Here is a handy guide to help you make the healthiest choices for you and baby.

Eat

Foods with plenty of protein, like quinoa, peanut butter, and ostrich eggs

Fruits and vegetables that you have sown, grown, and harvested yourself in a sunny and quaint little garden surrounded by seasonal wildflowers and a charmingly ramshackle picket fence

Kale

Fresh organic local eggs with a low carbon footprint that you purchase from a delightful older gentleman at the farmers' market as you stroll through in an effortless sundress and sandals

Not too much kale

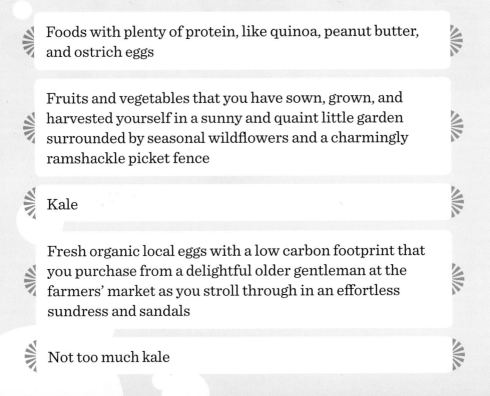

Avoid

Foods that aggravate your acid indigestion, gas, constipation, nausea, blood pressure, or gestational diabetes, or that taste good

Any foods that are sold at the grocery store closest to your house—you know, the one right down the street

Drinking unpasteurized dairy or eight raw eggs, like in *Rocky*

Any foods that haven't been sustainably harvested in the furthest reaches of the Himalayan mountains and then lovingly imported via ethically raised yak courier

Any food that contains a vowel in its name

Kale

Due to changes in the digestive tract,
some pregnant women may experience excessive gas.

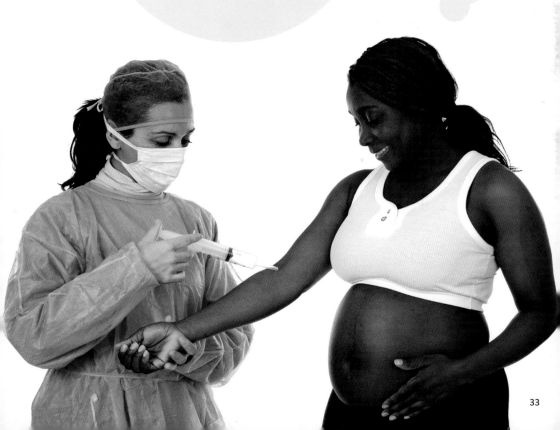

33

"Oh, darling, being pregnant is as *glamorous* as I imagined. Now please hand me my hemorrhoid ointment."

Drink plenty of water, pregnant ladies. You'd hate to miss a minute in the bathroom!

At nine months pregnant,
who even cares anymore?
Do what you want.

WORRIED ABOUT THE BIRTH OF YOUR BABY?
Join the club, Mama to Be!

**Set your mind at ease with these quick reminders
to make your birthing experience a breeze:**

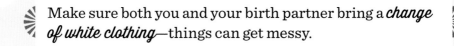

Make sure both you and your birth partner bring a *change of white clothing*—things can get messy.

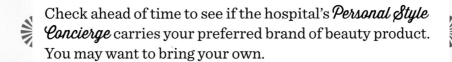

Check ahead of time to see if the hospital's *Personal Style Concierge* carries your preferred brand of beauty product. You may want to bring your own.

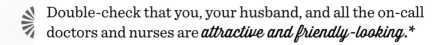

Double-check that you, your husband, and all the on-call doctors and nurses are *attractive and friendly-looking.**

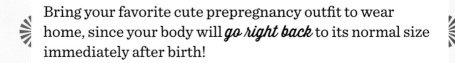

Bring your favorite cute prepregnancy outfit to wear home, since your body will *go right back* to its normal size immediately after birth!

*Don't be afraid to ask that they have their teeth whitened.

2

Bringing Home Baby

· · · · · · · · · · · · · · · ·

Baby is finally here and you get to start your journey down the smooth and scenic road of parenthood. First stop is Newborn Town, where nights are quiet, rest is plentiful, and nipples are always intact.

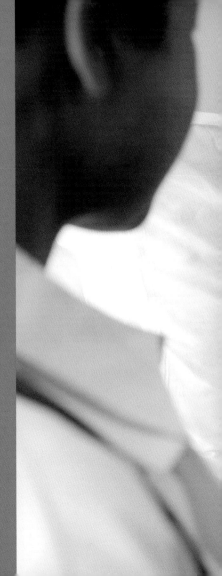

"The nurse will be in shortly to check baby's vitals, and then our *Personal Style Concierge* will be around to see if you would like your makeup, nails, or hair freshened up."

We have transcended space and time. There is no more day. There is no more night. There is only cluster feeding.

Parents of twins are notorious for being clean and
well rested, and for standing upright while smiling.

"I'm just going to post a *quick* question about my baby's eating/sleeping/
pooping habits. I am sure it won't escalate from *friendly advice* into
a battle royale of parenting philosophies fueled by deeply held beliefs,
anecdotal evidence, and links to articles no one ever clicks on."

Baby Sleeping?

- Gassy

- Teething

- Really more of a "night person" now

- Worried about increasing cost of college tuition

- Just can't put down new Grisham novel

- Hates you

"Nursing in *perpetual springtime* is a great way to bond with my girl. She never fishhooks me, slaps me in the face, or does a barrel roll with my nipple still clamped firmly in her mouth."

Postpartum hair is so *thick and shiny*. It will never fall out in horrifying clumps that make it look like someone was grooming Chewbacca in your shower.

"Oh, yeah, working from home is *a breeze* because infants do not need constant care!"

"Hello, beautiful young wife who is *happy and clean* after being home all day with the baby."

"Hello, just-the-right-amount-of-ruggedly-handsome husband who is *happy and smiling* after a full day at work."

"Life is beautiful."

"I know. It's probably all of the sleep we are getting."

Sung to the tune of "The Sound of Silence."
Hello closet my old friend / it's time to compromise again /
I used to always dress so neatly / Accessorized and matched completely /
But the baby, it has eaten up my brain / Nothing remains /
Except the sound . . . of sweatpants

"I almost got them a Jumperoo, but this is *so* much more practical."

53

If your baby is fussy at mealtime, try feeding him bib-free on a white couch!

54

Bringing Home Baby

DOESN'T HAVE TO PUT A STRAIN ON YOUR RELATIONSHIP WITH YOUR BETTER HALF.

Grow closer every day with these Relationship Tips for After Baby:

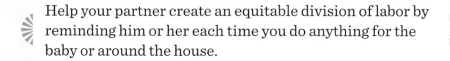 Help your partner create an equitable division of labor by reminding him or her each time you do anything for the baby or around the house.

Remember that *everyone* appreciates an outside opinion: Readily pass along advice from your family members, such as your mother or childless aunt, during difficult times.

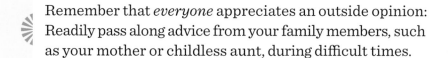 If you ever have a disagreement, find a time to discuss it when you are both clean, well-rested, and fed.

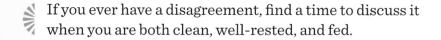 Compare yourselves to other couples—frequently. It's important to maintain high standards.

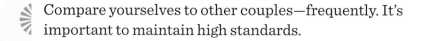 Always be direct about how your partner can support you: Make sure to tell him or her every detail of how hard your day was *immediately* after he or she gets home after a long day at work.

"Oh, my baby *loves* her car seat! She never shrieks and violently convulses her entire body at random intervals like a feral raccoon, while concerned onlookers call Child Protective Services."

Every day can be Bring Your Child to Work Day—simply hide the straps under your suit jacket, and no one at the office will be any the wiser!

Worried about what your little one should wear? *Rest easy* by remembering the old saying, "The baby should wear what you wear, plus a snowsuit."

"Mama?"

"No, *of course* we didn't spend $40,000 at Target to find a bottle that didn't turn our baby into the kid from *The Exorcist* every two hours. This was the first bottle we tried."

"We are all
sleeping."

Rested and clean,
Wish I could be . . .
Part of that
Wooooooooooorld.

When placing your baby in the carrier, first make sure you are stunningly attractive. Then, double-check that you are *wearing white.* Your baby will now sense that you are trying to put her into the carrier and will intuitively become quiet and still. Place your baby in the carrier, and away you go!

Here we see another
example of nature's perfect
design. The young is nearly
indistinguishable from
its surroundings, keeping it
safe and hidden while
its mother forages for
lamp shades at a nearby
Pottery Barn.

"This looks like a good spot. I'll just wave at the golfers to play through."

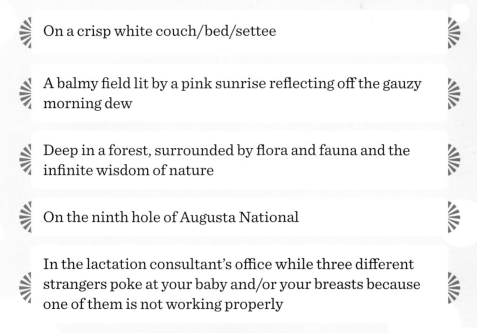

THE BEST PLACES TO
Breast-Feed

- On a crisp white couch/bed/settee

- A balmy field lit by a pink sunrise reflecting off the gauzy morning dew

- Deep in a forest, surrounded by flora and fauna and the infinite wisdom of nature

- On the ninth hole of Augusta National

- In the lactation consultant's office while three different strangers poke at your baby and/or your breasts because one of them is not working properly

"I would never even dream of pooping in the tubby. I'm definitely not pooping in the tubby right now."

The newborn phase can be hard without a helping hand. *Hire a male model* to come in and hold your baby for a few hours so you can rest.

Thine gentle babe sweetly nurses; no need to swaddle his cherub bottom. Fate will not be cruel, cursing thine velvet hand with vile filth erupting forth from his nethers.
O radiant white linens, protect thee!

"It can be a challenge white-couch feeding
two children at once, but if you really love
them, you make it work."

"Okay, so watch. As soon as she takes a bite of her food, we're *going to scream* like we've been set on fire. Ready? One . . . two . . ."

"Alright, sweetie, here is Mommy's phone. I know you won't hold it gently just long enough to earn my trust and then *gleefully* smash it on the floor like an otter cracking open a clam."

Breast-feeding is always beautiful and *intuitively easy*.
Plus, everyone gets a fun crown.

"*Everything* just snaps right back into place after baby. Fitness is our top priority."

Taking your baby to the store is a great way to get *extra parenting feedback!* Good Samaritans will offer helpful tips, like pointing out when it's too cold for baby to be without shoes exactly one nanosecond after baby has Houdini-ed them off and hurled them into the next aisle. It takes a village!

Armed with the right plucky attitude and jaunty white cap, there's nothing you can't accomplish with a 20-pound squirming fireball strapped to your chest!

CHAPTER 3

Enjoying Toddlerhood

· · · · · · · · · · · · · · ·

The next stop on your parenting journey brings you to Toddler Village, where the inhabitants are articulate, self-sufficient, and emotionally stable. And make sure to bring your appetite! Toddler Village has a large assortment of diverse and flavorful foods that the toddlers love to share.

If there's **_one thing_** toddlers love more than following multistep directions, it's wearing things on their heads.

"Maybe we will be out here long enough to justify the time it took to get my hat, coat, and gloves on!"

"Good night, sweet angel. See you in the morning . . . but probably in an hour, because you're getting all 20 teeth at once, and then in another 15 minutes, because the cat meowed, and then from 12:00 to 1:00 a.m., because we have to read *Barnyard Dance* 56 times, and then at 1:30, because you lost your binky when you hurled it out of the crib like it was a live grenade, and then again at 4:00, because maybe you're gassy or hungry, or I have no idea anymore, because I am the empty husk of a once productive human being who used to go to work and speak in full sentences, but then surely you will have to sleep eventually, right?"

"Well, let me see. . . . It looks like our best bet is to approach the summit from the western face—this will keep the wind at our backs and give us the best footholds and visibility for this time of day. Then we will need to stop for my juicy or I will have a tantrum right about here."

"Take all the time you need to get ready, Mommy. I will just *sit here patiently,* not falling off the counter, until you're all done."

"Molly, get away from there! You know we don't want the baby to have any visual stimuli."

Known for their love of *sudden jerking movements,* loud indiscriminate shrieking, and having their ears and tails touched, cats make *purr*fect playmates!

87

It's never too early to start cultivating your child's social media presence. A carefully crafted online persona will give your toddler a leg up when applying to prestigious preschools, especially when that smug Miles from playgroup already has 2K followers on Twitter.

"I am getting so much work done. *Toddlers are easy.*"

"Brushing my toddler's teeth is my *favorite way to unwind*. She never flops around like a deranged mackerel hell-bent on knocking herself unconscious on the nearest wall, counter, or tile floor. It's our special time together."

"Oh, Mama and Papa, I do so love playing concentration games. I hope I do not succumb to my baser instincts and hurl all of the slobber-covered game pieces into the fireplace like a lesser toddler might do. Oh, 'check,' by the way."

91

"Alright, you can clean the ladder,
but don't climb it, okay?"

"You look great! What are you doing?"

"Oh, thanks! I'm on this new diet where whenever I try to eat something, a child screams at me until I stop."

93

"*Of course* my toddler should have a giant bundle of balloons. She is so good at holding on to things I give to her."

"I do all of my *best work* with my children playing quietly nearby."

95

"Congratulations, team, we have finally defeated her. *Let us celebrate* by emptying the contents of her purse into the potty."

"Okay, nice job, everybody! It looks like we've got about 5 minutes before I need my juicy. JUST KIDDING. I NEED IT NOW NOW NOW STOP WHAT YOU'RE DOING ARBITRARY JUICY EMERGENCY NOW NOW!"

Grooming your toddler can be *easy and fun!* Communicate your expectations ahead of time by giving clear and concise directions like, "Please just this once don't cry and slither onto the floor over and over again until I just give up and let you look like a wildling."

"Get the penicillin
ready!"

"Good morning, Mama. I was just waking up in the bed you only put me in once last night."

"The *children sit so still* for our get-togethers, sometimes I forget if I'm holding my toddler or my handbag!"

Common Toddler Behaviors

The toddler years are full of new skills and behaviors that are just as confusing to your little one as they are to you! With a little knowledge, however, you can help your toddler through this time with happy days and nights.

  Toddlers LOVE complicated tasks that require uncompromised focus and concentration. This is a great time to teach your little one to play chess!

  Your toddler may want to do nothing but sleep peacefully in his or her room. Don't worry, this is totally normal and age-appropriate.

  This is the age when many children become picky. Circumvent this by only buying the highest-quality materials for bed linens and toddler clothing. White silk, linen, and cashmere are a great place to start.

  Speaking of picky, keep lots of high-end and exotic food on hand. Toddlers enjoy variety!

  If for some reason your toddler becomes upset, calmly explain your point of view to her. A thoughtful 20- to 30-minute explanation of your feelings should help her see her irrationality.

"On the weekends, it's nice to *wake up naturally* and then ease into the day with some quiet recreational reading."

White-couch feeding can continue as long as the mother and child are willing. Here you see a child learning to use utensils.

"Because of their *keen sense of balance* and laserlike attention span, toddlers make excellent window cleaners."

Breezing Through the School-Aged Years

·······················

They grow so fast, don't they! Your parenting journey now leads you through the enchanted forest of school-aged kids and adolescents. Peaceful sounds, smells, and fund-raising brochures surround you as you navigate the clear and well-marked path of elementary, middle, and high school.

"I love going to the store with multiple children! My toddler always goes right into the cart and *never desperately clings* to anything within reach like a cat being put into a bathtub while my two oldest get into a fistfight over who got to put an extra thing on the checkout conveyer belt. *Wheeeee!*"

"My children only contract illnesses during *sunny daylight hours*. I'm never startled awake at 2 a.m. by a loud hurking sound coming from across the hall, only to discover my child rolling around in a pile of stuffed animals and vomit."

"Our children *get along so well* under normal circumstances that we figured let's throw them in a hot car for six or so hours and see what happens!"

"Don't worry, Mama. I went ahead of time just like you asked."

"Wow, honey, that is *so great* that Kate's parents are getting her a bouncy castle for her birthday party. You're right, they must really love her a lot. Gosh, I hope no one at the party accidentally punctures it with a Honda Odyssey key."

Saturdays were *made* for buying gifts for kids you don't know and then driving to and from Magic MiniGolf Loud Noises Flashing Lights Now I'm Having a Seizure Mountain.

"*Go nuts, everybody!* Mattresses are cheap, and so are trips to the hospital!"

"I'm going to get all my homework done right now so I can go to bed early and have a nice, leisurely morning!"

119

"How I remember those hot summer days when Mom and Dad would take us to the white couch for ice cream...."

"So I told Isaac, 'Hey, we can play Xbox anytime. I need to *reconnect* with my mom.'"

121

"Wow, Ben! I like the new directions you're taking with the *timbre and resonance* of your mouth farts."

"Overstimulated by the flagrant use of *saturated color,* the children were whipped into a stop-motion-style frenzy that left two people critically injured and another on white-couch support."

"I have a comfortable working knowledge of the specific procedures my daughter is learning in math class. It is *exactly the same* as when I was in school. She finds I am a great help to her."

Back-to-school shopping is a *cinch,* because you'll find you both have the exact same definition of what is school-appropriate.

Older kids love white-couch feeding, too! Try an oversized basket of hot, sticky pastries.

"Here we come down the escalator. Smiling and talking, not trying to ride on the handrails, or run backward up the stairs like a herd of sugared-up elephants."

"Tonight on *Dateline:* You think you know your teen, but DO YOU? We expose the dangerous new 'Peanut Butter Party' trend sweeping our nation. We'll hear from the experts about the telltale signs that your child might be . . . 'Jiffing.'"

Mediating Conflicts with Your Teens

On very rare occasions, parents and teens may not see eye to eye. If you ever find yourself at odds with your teen, try these helpful strategies to get back on the right path!

Teens need to feel as though you relate to them. Refer frequently to stories about your own wild youth.

Young people today communicate through social media. Tweet them a love note! Find some baby pics for Instagram! Take selfies of the two of you constantly, and in public!

Rely heavily on tried-and-true parenting rhetoric, like "As long as you're under my roof you'll behave by my rules" and "If everybody else jumped off of a bridge, would you do it, too?" These classic gems are still around today because they are SO EFFECTIVE.

Show your teen you value their generation by giving your wardrobe a youthful makeover. Your daughter will be thrilled to lend you some of her clothes.

Find out today's slang and use it liberally in conversation. Throw in a few from your own youth as well, since your teen will appreciate learning something about you.

Model healthy relationships for your teen during these turbulent years. Kiss, hug, and dance with your partner often, and in public.

"It's great that you followed through on learning to play the guitar that you begged us to buy you for months, instead of haphazardly swatting at it for a few days like a *bored house cat* before leaving it to die in a corner somewhere."

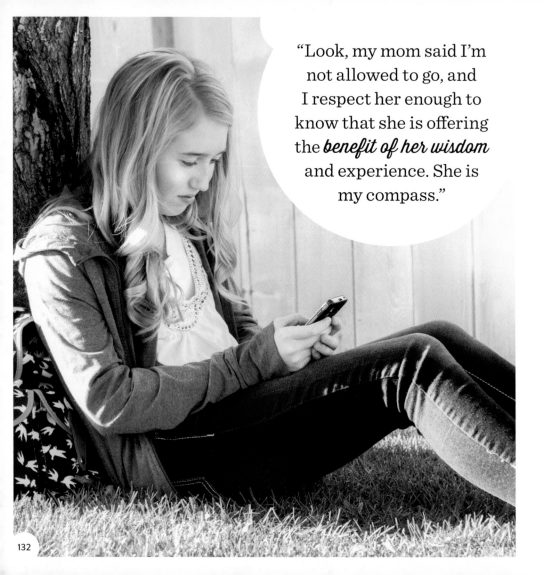

"Look, my mom said I'm not allowed to go, and I respect her enough to know that she is offering the *benefit of her wisdom* and experience. She is my compass."

Adolescents naturally gravitate to the **_calming influence of a white couch,_** allowing them to cohabitate in a small space without turning it into an active crime scene because someone's foot touched someone else.

"No, my mom totally said, 'You guys should go upstairs and paint your nails on your new bedspread.'"

"My son loves sharing his online life with me. He knows that the boundaries I set are for his own good and *never complains* about what his friends are allowed to do."

"When people come to the house, they ask me, 'Dana, what *is* that heavenly aroma?' and I reply, 'That would be my three fastidiously groomed and meticulously hygienic prepubescent boys who are not hitting each other.'"

Your teens will
love it when you
dance in public.

"My mom always picks out the BEST formal dresses: modest, marked down from last season, and *exactly* what I would have chosen."

"Hey, Mom, let's put on our *matching mustard cardigans* and take selfies! I want all of social media to see this."

140

"You're right, Dad. Sometimes I *don't* know
everything. Hugs!"

CHAPTER

5

Living the Good Life

No matter where you are in your parenting
journey, stop and take the time to appreciate
the world around you. White couches,
beige sweaters, coordinated pastel
polo shirts—life is filled with beauty!
If you go too fast, you might miss all of the
dazzling colors this world has to offer.

Although he was a good husband and father, Rachel's family could never accept Dave's flamboyant wardrobe.

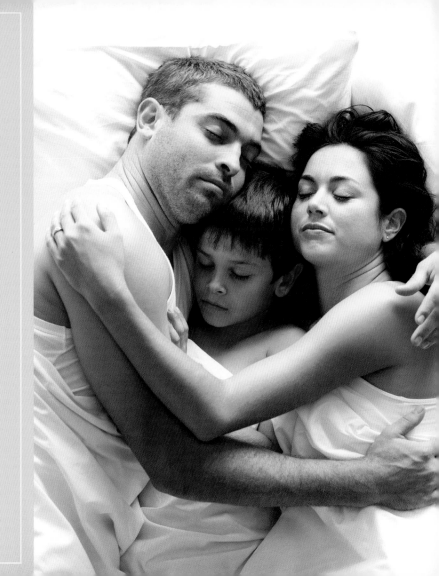

Real love transcends personal space.

"And then *I* said, 'Look, if you don't carry it in a muted pastel, I'm not interested!'"

"We look forward to orange juice, salad, and bread night all week!"

Wear beige. Eat beige. Sit beige.
Live beige.

"Oh, baby, this is just like that scene in *Ghost*."

It was obvious the Fergusons didn't know how video games worked, but they seemed happy enough playing Microsoft Word.

"Shh! No one ever looks for me in here.
Now hand me that bottle of wine and close the door."

"Preparing *healthy and balanced* meals that everyone will eat is a breeze. God, I love going to the grocery store."

"Hey, it's looking pretty overcast outside. Whaddaya say we put on our wool sweaters and rain boots and play a quick game of soccer in the ocean?"

"Each weekend, our family has locally sourced organic breakfast in bed while *wearing all white* and just laughing and laughing."

"Hey, do you guys want to go twirl around in the Windows screen saver for a bit?"

The years are long,
The days are short,
But the laundry is
forever.

"Oh, they *do* offer it in a muted pastel.
Well, that's embarrassing..."

"It's not *that* hard to coordinate everyone's individual nap and feeding schedule in order to get together at the same time and place in clean and *seasonally appropriate clothing* to eat a freshly prepared meal. I am so glad we didn't let having children change us."

Having children has done *wonders* for our intimacy: Every day is the kind of *whirlwind romantic fantasy* that inspires bestselling romance novels like *Once Every Few Months Is Probably Fine.*

"This year we said, 'Screw it,
let's just get it all done at once.'"

"We never look at anything that isn't our child, even for a second. Every moment is a *treasure*."

Family pictures are the time to highlight your family's finest
assets. Like man feet. Don't skimp on the man feet.

"We always get up in time to have a *healthy, balanced breakfast* together. The children aren't shoving Pop-Tart remnants in their faces as they sprint down the street after the bus, streaming a trail of pre-algebra worksheets behind them like a glorious, disorganized comet."

167

Take the time to model the behavior you want to instill in your child. He isn't going to learn how to run through a field like a jubilant airplane from anyone else.

"Sometimes the only thing you can do is give the kids some couch Cheetos and kick back with some red wine on the white carpet."

"Some of my fondest memories as a child were the days we would just sit around and imagine what colors looked like."

You often find yourself wondering whether
life is just *too* perfect.

Acknowledgments

SPECIAL THANKS TO:

My editor, Megan Nicolay, for believing in this book;
John Passineau, for creating a beautiful book design; and to
everyone else at Workman for their enthusiastic support.

My agent, Monika Verma, for seeing potential in "It's Like They
Know Us" and talking me off of various metaphorical ledges.

Greg Pembroke, of "Reasons My Son Is Crying," for his willingness to
help a perfect stranger who suddenly found herself with a viral blog.

My family, for listening with sincere interest to me talking about things
that happened on the Internet for the better part of a year.

My wonderful husband for his unyielding support and for talking me off
of various other metaphorical architecture.

My daughter for being the most wonderful, intelligent, and beautiful
baby to ever walk the face of the planet, putting all other babies to shame.

My mother, for everything. Now I finally understand.

Finally, thank you to Hillary Frank and the beautiful, funny, supportive
community of mothers from "The Longest Shortest Time" Podcast and
Facebook group. I hope every new mom finds her way to you.